Robins

GEORGE K. PECK

SMART APPLE MEDIA

Published by

Smart Apple Media

123 South Broad Street

Mankato, Minnesota 56001

⚜

Copyright © 1998 Smart Apple Media.

International copyrights reserved in all countries.

No part of this book may be reproduced in any form without

written permission from the publisher.

Printed in the United States of America.

Photos by George K. Peck,

Robert McCaw, David Dvorak Jr.,

Kurt Thorson / Hillstrom Stock Photo, Inc.,

Anthony Mercieca, Richard Jacobs / Root Resources / Hillstrom Stock Photo, Inc.

Editorial assistance by Barbara Ciletti

Library of Congress Cataloging-in-Publication Data

Peck, George K.

Robins / written by George Peck.

p. cm.

Includes index.

Summary: Describes the life cycle, behavior, and habitat

of this songbird.

ISBN 1-887068-11-2

1. Robins—Juvenile literature. [1. American robin. 2. Robins] I. Title.

QL696.P288P435   1998   96-19422

598.8'42—dc20   CIP

                                                                              AC

First Edition   5 4 3 2 1

C O N T E N T S

The Robin is the one

That interrupts the morn

With hurried, few,

express reports

that March is early on

-Emily Dickinson

How do we know that spring has sprung?

Some people go by their calendars, counting off the days. Others say that spring has arrived when the last snowdrift melts, or when the first green tulip leaves poke up from the frozen earth.

But for many people, the surest sign of spring is the appearance of the American Robin on lawns and in trees across North America. When we see our first robin of the season, we know that winter is truly gone. Even the robin's familiar song—*cheerup, cheerup, cheerily*—seems to welcome the change of seasons.

When English settlers came to America in the 17th century, they saw a handsome orange-breasted bird with a lovely song. It reminded them of a small European thrush called the Robin. They named the American bird after its European cousin. The American Robin, like the European Robin, is a member of the thrush family.

There are 306 species of thrushes. Thrushes live on every continent except Antarctica and can be found in a variety of habitats. The White-necked Thrush lives in the tropical rain forests of South America. The Desert Wheatear survives in the scorching, arid heat of the Sahara Desert, and the Gray-cheeked Thrush prefers northern evergreen forests. Twenty different species of thrushes are found in North America, including the Wood Thrush, the Hermit Thrush, and the colorful Eastern Bluebird.

Of all the North American thrush species, the American Robin is the most familiar and the most widespread. During the winter, robins live in Central America, Mexico, the islands of the Caribbean, and in the southern United States. During the summer months they can be found throughout the continental United States and Canada. Robins live in many different habitats including woodlands, shrubby grasslands, mountains, and even the treeless tundra of northern Canada.

But most of us know the robin from its favorite habitat—city parks, gardens, orchards, and our own backyards.

American Robin in Aspen spring snowfall.

Most thrushes are medium-sized birds. They vary from the tiny Rufous-breasted Bush-Robin of southwest China and Tibet which is 4 1/2 inches (11 cm) long, to the Great Thrush from the mountains of Venezuela and Bolivia which is 13 inches (33 cm) long. The Bush-Robin is the same size as the familiar chickadee, and the Great Thrush is almost as long as our Common Grackle.

The American Robin is 10 inches (25 cm) long. It is the largest North American thrush. The robin legs and feet are designed for walking or hopping on level ground, or gripping a tiny branch high in a tree. Its beak is long and pointed, but not as long as a hummingbird's beak, and not as pointed as a blackbird's.

Like its smaller cousin the European Robin, the American Robin is known for its deep orange-red breast. Its back and wings are dark gray, with a darker head and tail. It has a white-streaked chin, incomplete white rings around the eyes, and a yellow beak with a black tip. The robin's belly, between and behind the legs, is white. The outer tail feathers of eastern robins usually have white tips, but in the west the tail can be solid gray.

Male and female robins look very much alike. The males may have brighter breast feathers and a darker head, but unless you see a pair of robins together, it can be hard to tell which is which.

Young American Robins look similar to their parents, but their orange breasts are speckled with black, and their backs are streaked or mottled.

Two Mexican species which are found in the southern United States, the Clay-colored Robin and the Rufous-backed Robin, look like robins that have been colored using the wrong crayons! The Clay-colored Robin has a tawny, yellowish breast and brownish-olive upper parts. The Rufous-backed Robin has a light gray head, tail, and wings, with brownish-red shoulders, breast, and back.

Eastern and Western Bluebirds, two other members of the thrush family, also have red-orange breasts. But with their bright blue backs and wings, you could never mistake a bluebird for a robin!

In the late summer, when the breeding season is over, adult robins lose their old feathers and grow new winter plumage. This yearly shedding and growth of new feathers is called molting. The new breast feathers are edged in white, and the feathers on the head are lighter in color. This fresh new plumage is worn during the winter. In the spring, when the robins return to their northern breeding grounds, the white edges of the new feathers will have worn away, once again making the breast a bright orange-red color.

Watch closely the next time you spy a robin on your lawn. It will stand perfectly still and tilt its head to the side, the way you do when you want to hear a very soft sound. Many people say that it listens for the sound of moving worms. But the robin isn't listening. It is tipping its head so it can see better. When a worm peeks out of its hole, the robin quickly snatches it with its strong beak and gobbles it down.

Earthworms are one of the robin's favorite foods, but this bird is not a fussy diner. Like other members of the thrush family, the American Robin enjoys a wide variety of fruits, insects, and other invertebrates. Grasshoppers, beetles, ants, termites, caterpillars, spiders, or small snails—if it crawls on the ground, it might taste good to a hungry robin. Robins like fruit too—especially berries. They eat cherries, Juneberries, dogwood berries, and bayberries. If there is no other food around, robins will feed on apples or other large fruit.

American Robin feeding on worm.

Because thrushes feed on fresh fruit and insects, they cannot survive the harsh winters of the northern United States and Canada. Like most other birds that breed in the temperate regions of the world, thrushes must fly south for the winter. This twice-a-year movement—from north to south in the fall, and back again in the spring—is called migration.

Robins that live in moderate climates such as northern California or the southeastern United States might not migrate at all. But as the weather begins to turn cold in the northern regions, most American Robins begin to gather into small flocks for their journey south. They have been eating well all summer long, building up their reserves of body fat. They have a thick layer of new feathers to keep them warm. But by the time the first snowflakes fall, the robins are headed south, flying both by night and by day.

The robin is a strong flyer, but its top speed is only about 35 miles per hour (56 kph). The journey from north to south might take as long as a month. Some robins travel as far south as Central America. Others spend their winters in the southern United States and Mexico.

In late winter, robins feel the urge to return to their northern homelands, where they were born. The males leave first, flying north in February or early March, following the spring thaw. Sometimes a male robin will travel too far north, too soon. It is a sorry sight to see an early robin pecking at the frozen earth, searching for food. In this case the early bird doesn't get the worm!

But there is a good reason why the male robins want to get home as soon as possible. The sooner they can claim a territory up north, the better their chances of finding a mate.

About one month after the male robins arrive at their northern breeding grounds, they begin to sing. Their cheerful song—*cheerup, cheerup, cheerily*—is heard morning and evening, from April until midsummer.

Why do robins sing? Is it because they are happy to see warm weather again? Is it to entertain us? The fact is, male robins start singing because the female robins have begun to arrive. It is time to defend a territory and to find a mate.

The male's song contains two messages. It tells other male robins, "Stay away! This is my territory!" A robin's territory is not very large—usually only about one-third of an acre—but its boundaries are very important to the robin. Male robins attack any other male robin that crosses that line. Some male robins have been known to attack their own reflections in windows, thinking they are fending off an invader.

The robin's song is also an invitation to female robins. "Look at me! I am strong and beautiful! I have claimed this fine territory for you!" When a female robin appears, the male pursues her, sometimes performing a short ground display, until she agrees to mate with him.

Once the male and female robin mate, they search for a nest site together. Most robins build their nests in the crotches of tree branches, usually from 4 1/2 to 10 feet (1.4 to 3 m) above the ground. They also may nest on tree stumps, on ledges or windowsills, and occasionally on the ground. Robins may often choose nesting sites that give them a good view of their territory, and of approaching danger.

Other thrushes, such as the Hermit Thrush and the Veery, hide their nests on or near the ground, or at the base of bushes. Bluebirds are unusual—they are the only thrushes to nest in cavities. Many years ago, bluebirds nested in holes in trees. Today many of the available tree holes have been taken over by the aggressive European Starling. Most bluebirds now depend on handmade boxes for their nests. Bluebird boxes are now a common sight on fence poles all across the United States.

It takes a pair of robins from two to six days to build a nest. Both the male and the female gather nesting material, but the female builds the nest herself. She begins with weeds and grass. Then she gathers mud a beakful at a time and forms the nest into the shape of a cup. The grass and mud dry together, making a hard shell that looks a lot like a small cereal bowl. She lines the inside with a layer of soft fine grass, and the new home is ready.

The mother robin usually lays a clutch of three or four eggs. Each egg is oval and about an inch long. Robin eggs are famous for their beautiful color.

Usually the eggs are solid light blue, but on rare occasions they are flecked with brown spots. The next time you hear of a color called "robin's-egg blue," you'll know why.

The mother sits on the eggs for 11 to 14 days, keeping them warm and safe from harm while the father stays nearby, protecting their territory.

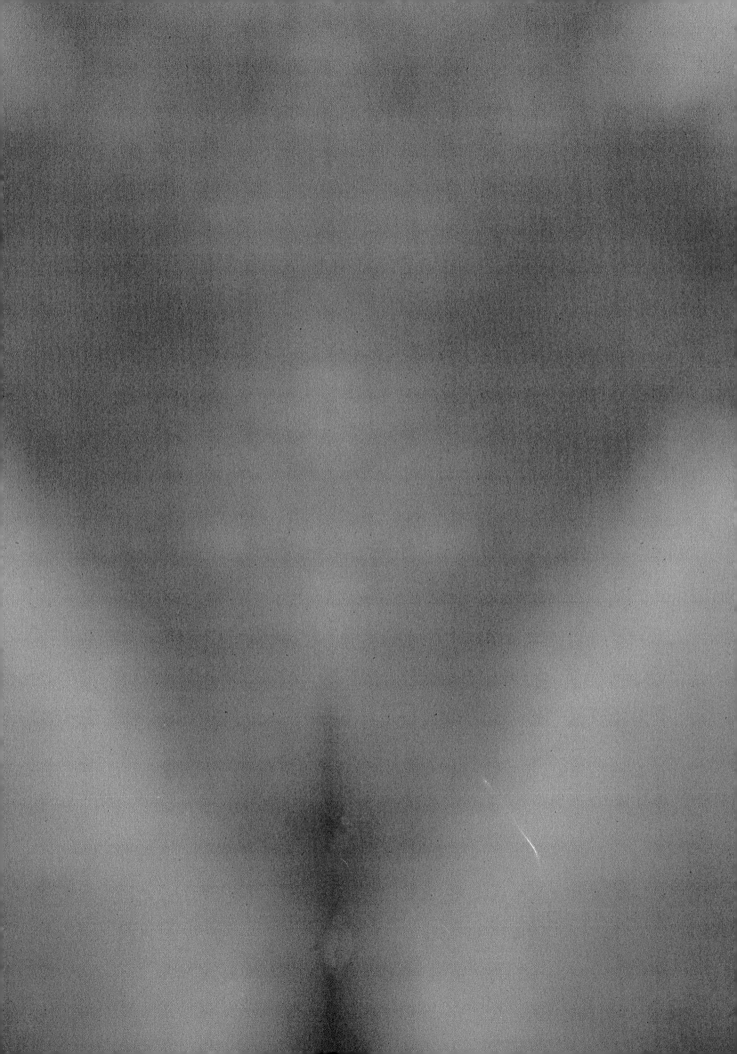

Baby robins hatch from their eggs blind, naked, and helpless. They have only a fine coating of down and must be kept warm at all times. The female keeps the babies covered, warming them with her body.

Robin chicks grow quickly and need to eat often. The mother and father take turns finding food. The hungry babies open wide, and the parents shove the food into their mouths. As the babies get bigger they are fed worms and larger insects.

Within two weeks, they are fully feathered and ready to leave the nest. Sometimes these fledgling robins jump out of the nest a little too soon. You might see a baby robin hopping about on the grass, unable to fly, peeping for its parents to bring it food.

Once the fledglings have left the nest, the male parent continues to feed and protect them. The female may return to the same nest to lay a new clutch of eggs. Robins may raise two or even three families a year.

Young robins will follow their father until they are able to find enough food on their own. Toward the end of the summer, the fledglings molt their speckled body feathers and grow their first winter plumage. They will fly south, like their parents, for the winter. When they return in the spring, they will be full-grown adults, ready to raise families of their own.

Hermit Thrush nest and young.

To an earthworm or a beetle, a hungry robin is a dangerous predator. Robins, in turn, are preyed upon by other creatures. Hawks, domestic cats, and other predators will attack and kill robins. House sparrows and starlings have been known to follow robins and steal earthworms from them. Climbing snakes will take young robins from their nest.

Migration is also a dangerous time. A snowstorm or a sudden cold snap might cause many migrating robins to die. Robins, as well as other songbirds, are threatened by people too. Feeding on a lawn that has been treated with weedkillers or pesticides can cause them to get sick and die. Some robins are killed by speeding cars, or by flying into windows.

Robins, like most small creatures, do not have very long lives. Most do not survive past their second year. But if a robin is lucky enough to avoid accidents, predators, and disease, it might live for as long as 11 years. One robin in captivity lived for 17 years!

Birds adapt to human development in a variety of ways. Many wild species avoid people and can only be found far from our cities and homes.

A few European species—pigeons, sparrows, and starlings—have adapted all too well. They are so common that some consider them pests.

The American Robin is one of the few native birds to thrive in our urban and suburban environments. In its natural environment, the robin and its relatives in the thrush family play an important role in the balance of nature. They help plant new fruit trees by eating berries and excreting the undigested seeds, and they eat millions of insects every day, helping to control harmful insect populations. Perhaps most important to us, the robin brings the beauty of nature into our parks, lawns, and gardens by singing its cheery song, strutting across the green grass, and showing off its proud orange breast.

I N D E X